More Andrew Lloyd Webber™ Piano Solos

ISBN 978-1-4234-8396-0

7777 W. BLUEMOUND RD. P.O. BOX 13819 MILWAUKEE, WI 53213

Visit Hal Leonard Online at
www.halleonard.com

AMIGOS PARA SIEMPRE
(Friends for Life)
(The Official Theme of the Barcelona 1992 Games)

Music by ANDREW LLOYD WEBBER
Lyrics by DON BLACK

Gentle Habanera feel

7

rall.   *a tempo*

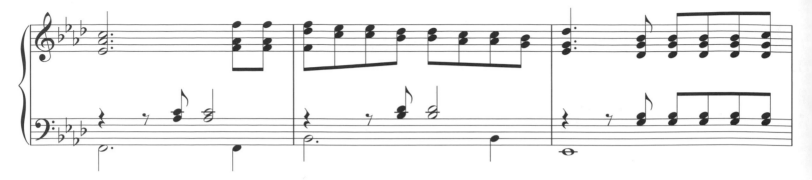

molto rall.   *meno mosso*

rall. molto al fine   **ff** *a tempo*

ANGEL OF MUSIC
from THE PHANTOM OF THE OPERA

Music by ANDREW LLOYD WEBBER
Lyrics by CHARLES HART
Additional Lyrics by RICHARD STILGOE

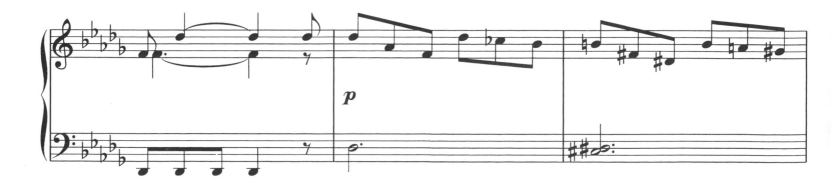

ANOTHER SUITCASE IN ANOTHER HALL

from EVITA

Words by TIM RICE
Music by ANDREW LLOYD WEBBER

Slow 8 beat ballad

With pedal

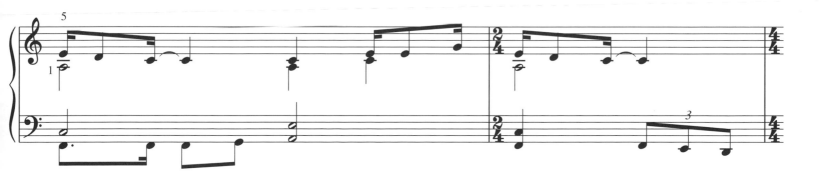

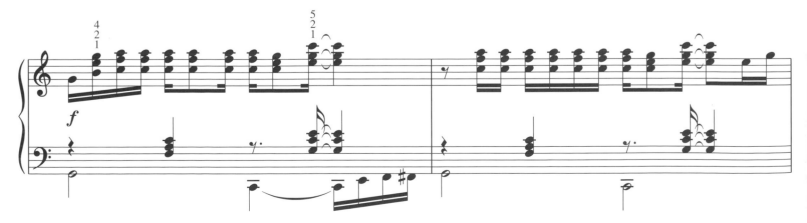

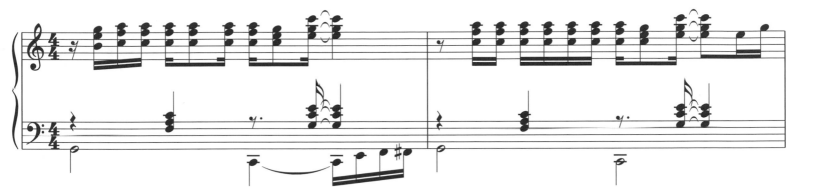

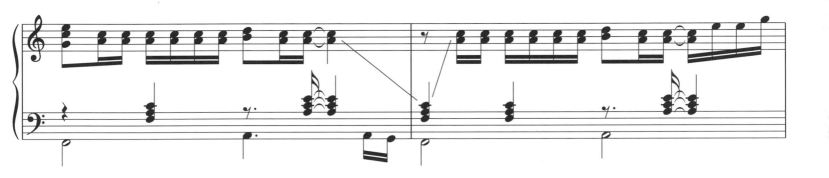

GUS: THE THEATRE CAT

from CATS

Music by ANDREW LLOYD WEBBER
Text by T.S. ELIOT

D.S. al Coda

CODA

Più mosso

Meno mosso

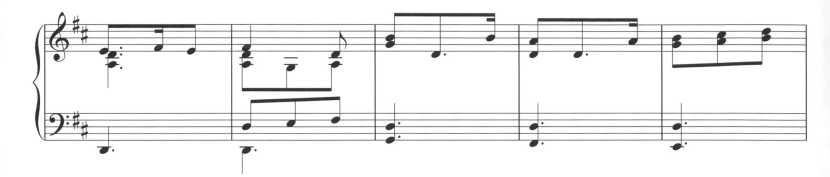

LEARN TO BE LONELY
from THE PHANTOM OF THE OPERA

Music by ANDREW LLOYD WEBBER
Lyrics by CHARLES HART

Moderato rubato

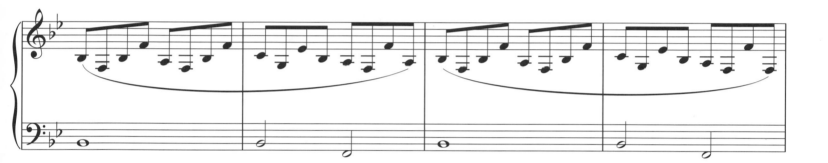

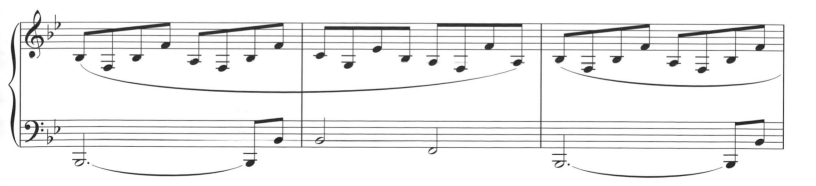

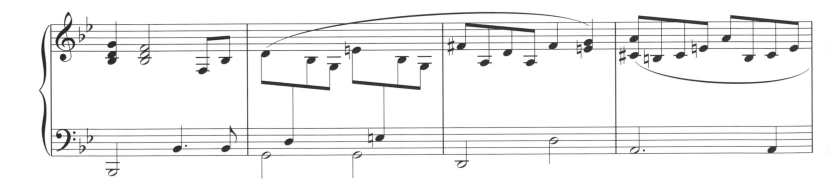

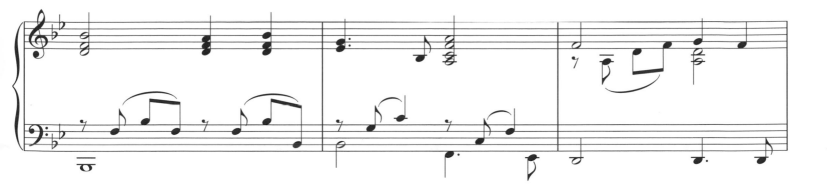

I BELIEVE MY HEART

from THE WOMAN IN WHITE

Music by ANDREW LLOYD WEBBER
Lyrics by DAVID ZIPPEL

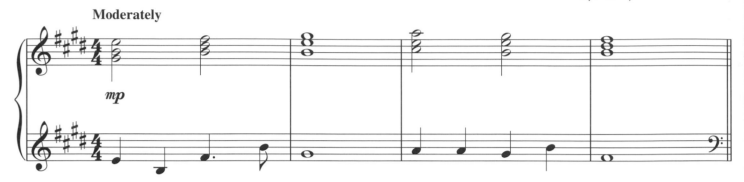

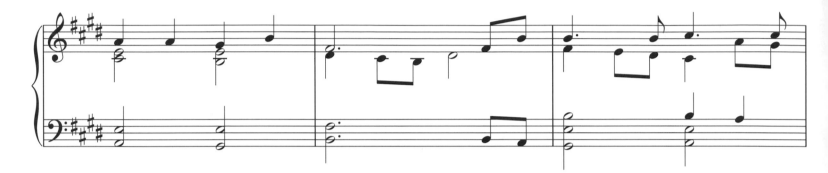

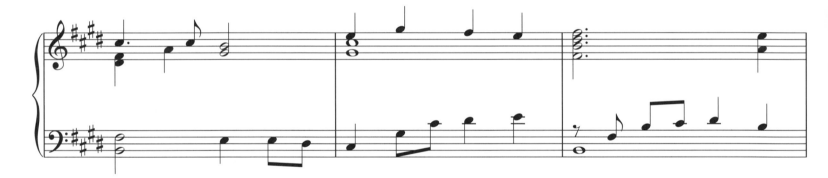

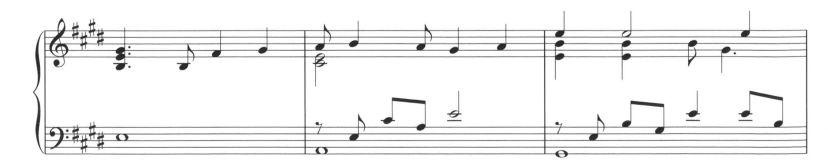

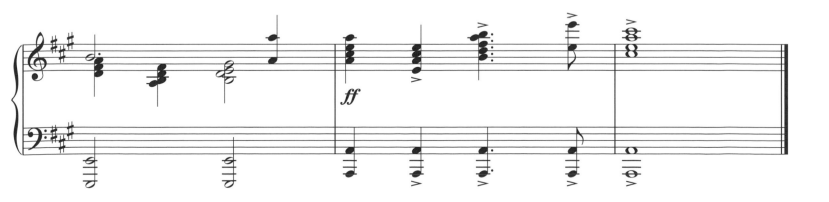

LOVE CHANGES EVERYTHING

from ASPECTS OF LOVE

Music by ANDREW LLOYD WEBBER
Lyrics by DON BLACK and CHARLES HART

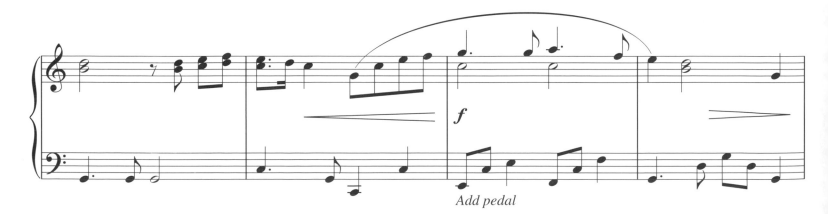

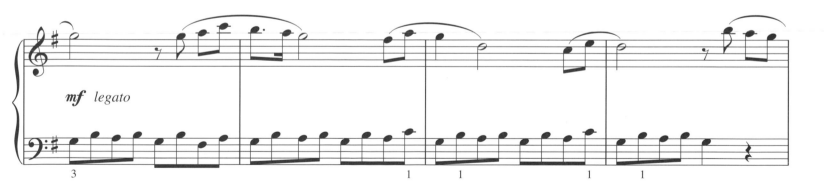

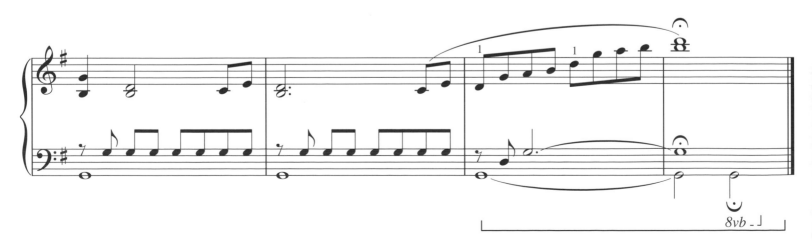

THE PERFECT YEAR
from SUNSET BOULEVARD

Music by ANDREW LLOYD WEBBER
Lyrics by DON BLACK and CHRISTOPHER HAMPTON

Moderato

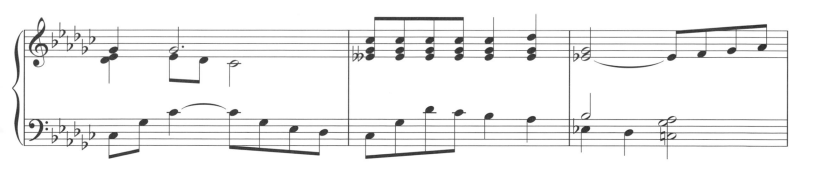

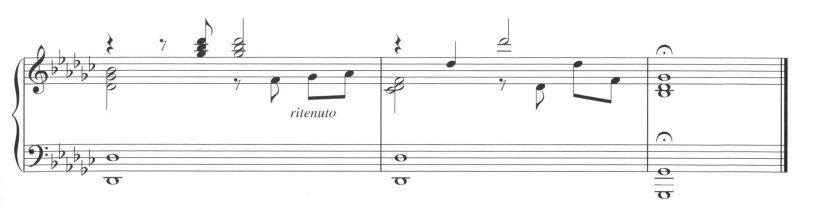

ritenuto

ONLY YOU

from STARLIGHT EXPRESS

Music by ANDREW LLOYD WEBBER
Lyrics by RICHARD STILGOE

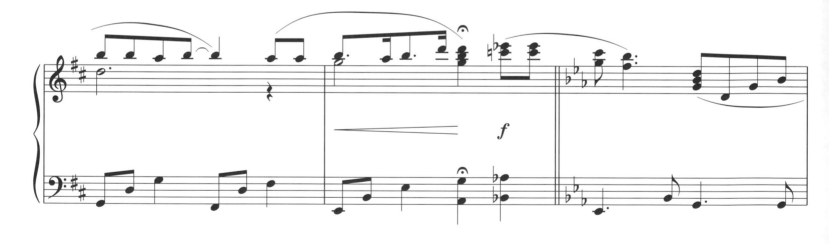

SEEING IS BELIEVING

from ASPECTS OF LOVE

Music by ANDREW LLOYD WEBBER
Lyrics by DON BLACK and CHARLES HART

Andante con moto

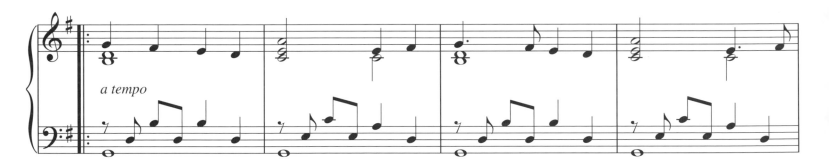

ten.

rit.   u tempo

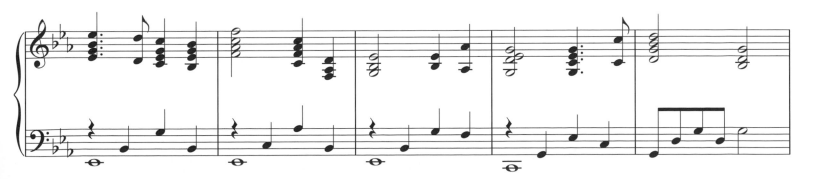

48

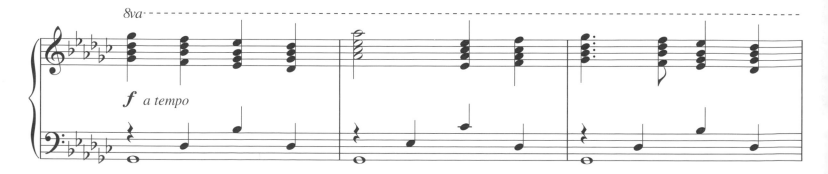

50

Tempo primo

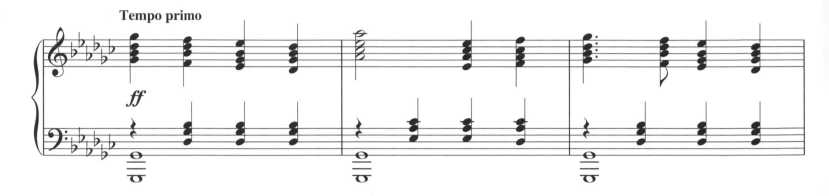

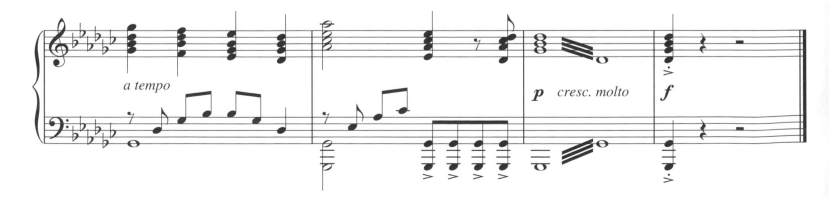

THINK OF ME
from THE PHANTOM OF THE OPERA

Music by ANDREW LLOYD WEBBER
Lyrics by CHARLES HART
Additional Lyrics by RICHARD STILGOE

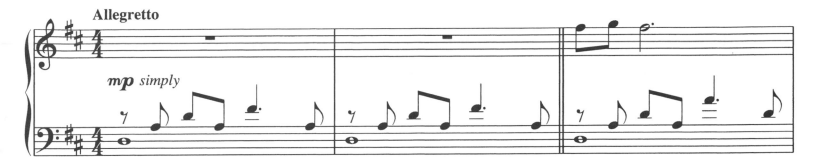

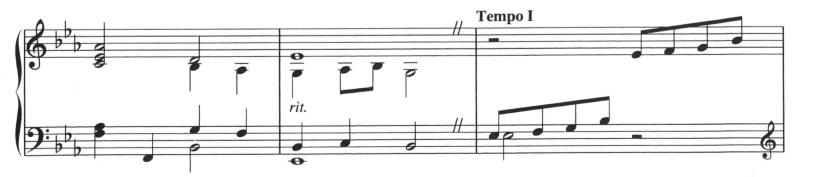

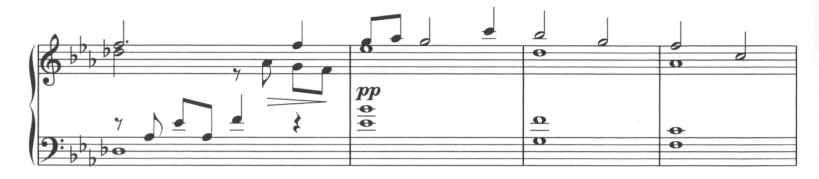

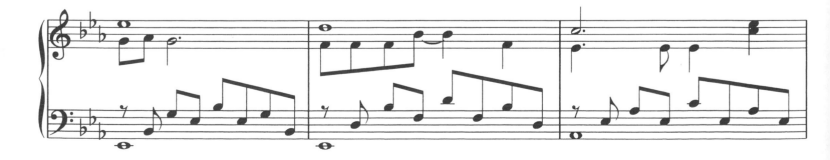

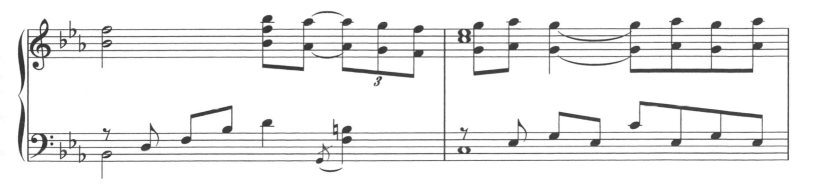

8va basso

SKIMBLESHANKS: THE RAILWAY CAT
from CATS

Music by ANDREW LLOYD WEBBER
Text by T.S. ELIOT

Bright

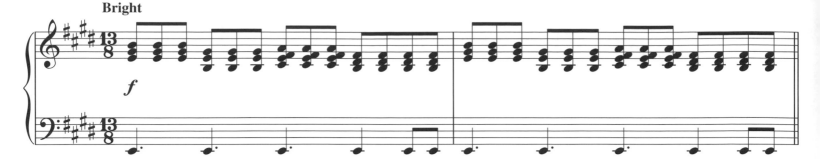

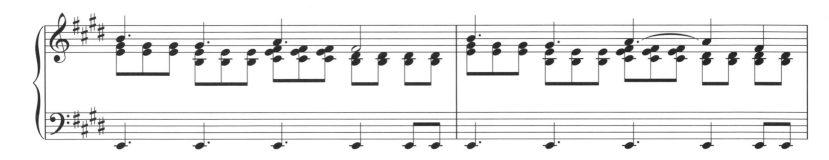

Quick

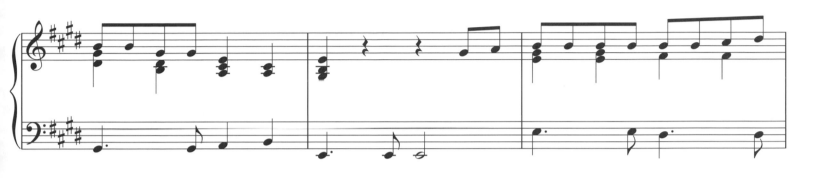

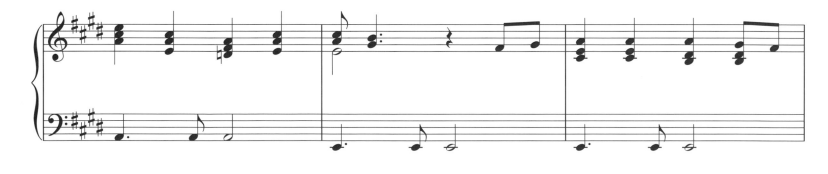

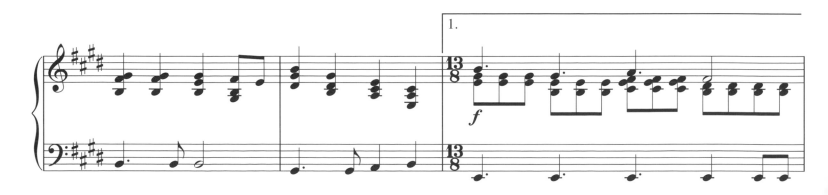

2.
Funky

1.

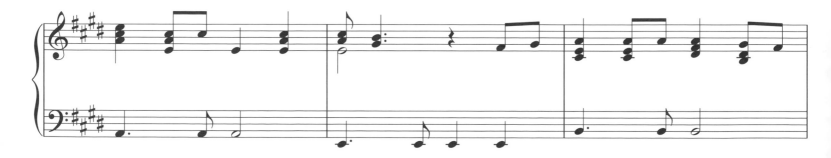

Quick

rall. molto

STARLIGHT EXPRESS

from STARLIGHT EXPRESS

Music by ANDREW LLOYD WEBBER
Lyrics by RICHARD STILGOE

Moderately slow

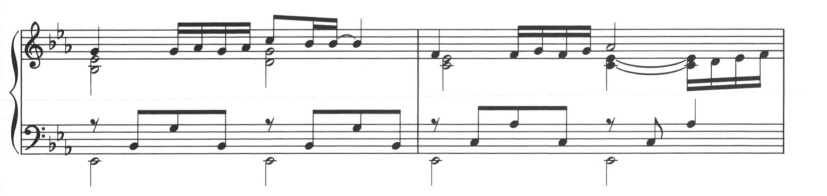

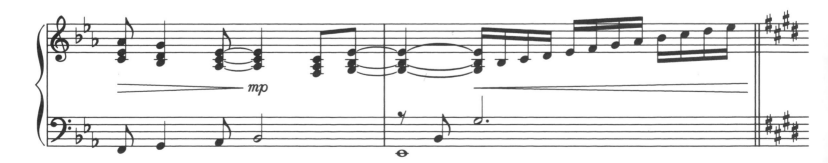

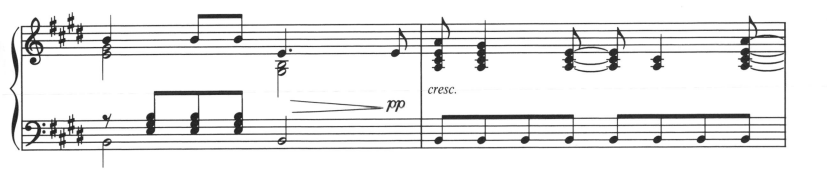

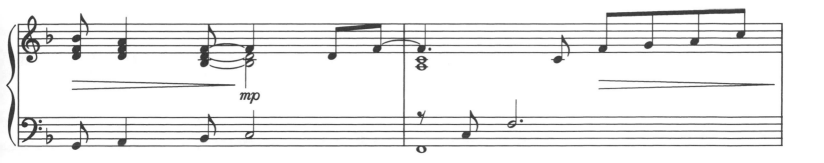

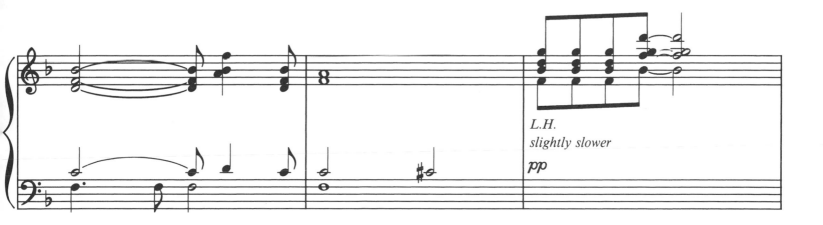

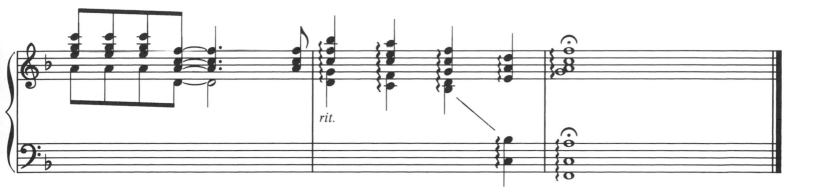

SUPERSTAR
from JESUS CHRIST SUPERSTAR

Words by TIM RICE
Music by ANDREW LLOYD WEBBER

Slowly

With pedal

Lively Rock

No pedal

simile

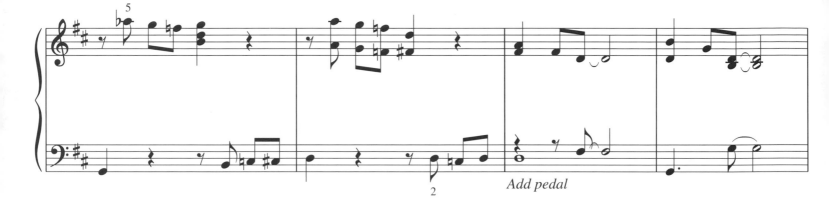

Repeat and Fade

TAKE THAT LOOK OFF YOUR FACE

from SONG & DANCE

Music by ANDREW LLOYD WEBBER
Lyrics by DON BLACK

Moderately

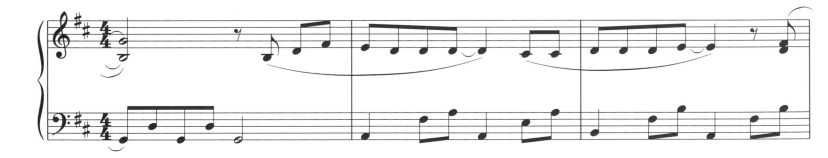

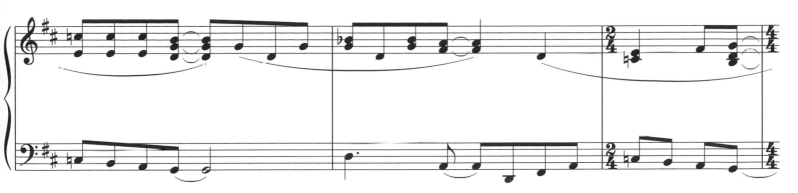

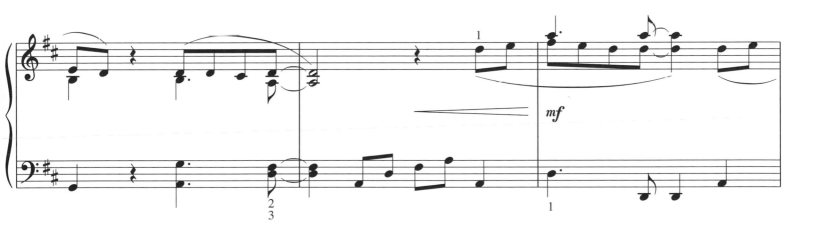

WISHING YOU WERE SOMEHOW HERE AGAIN

from THE PHANTOM OF THE OPERA

Music by ANDREW LLOYD WEBBER
Lyrics by CHARLES HART
Additional Lyrics by RICHARD STILGOE

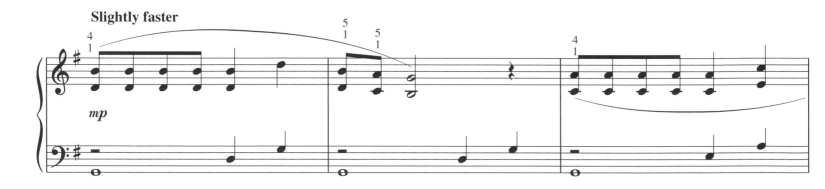

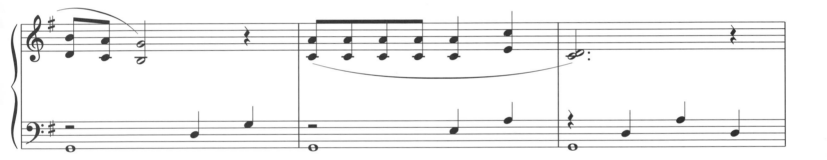

Slowly

rit.

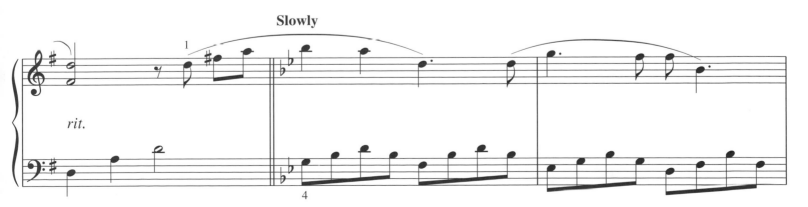

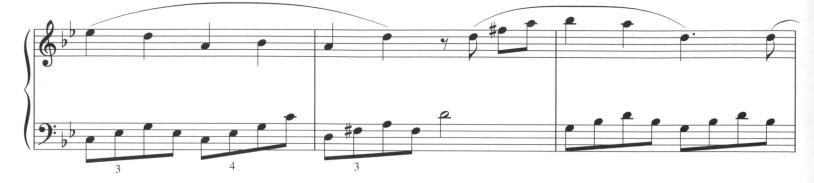

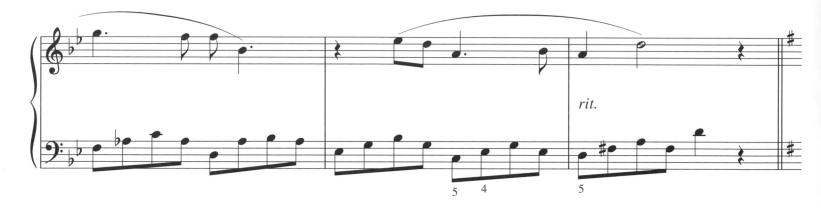

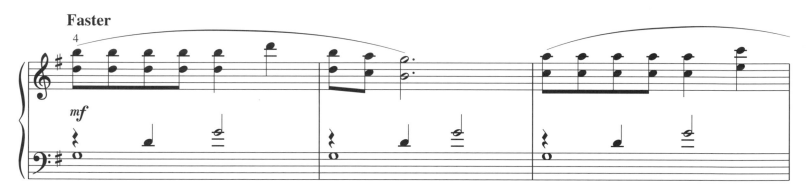

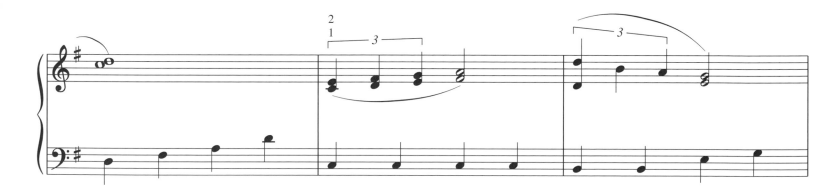

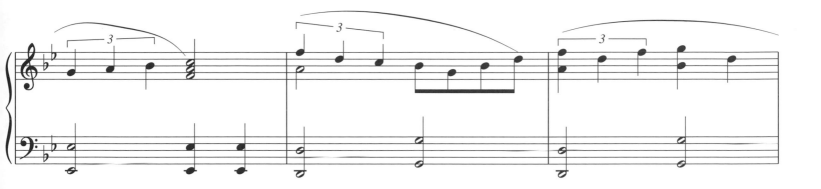

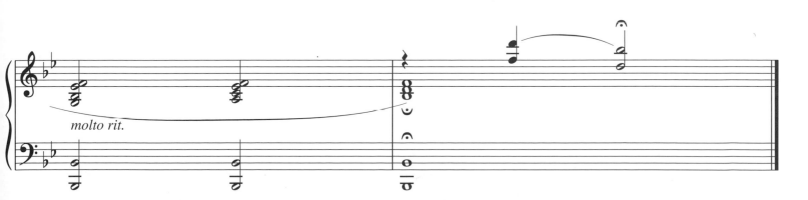

YOU MUST LOVE ME

from the Cinergi Motion Picture EVITA

Words by TIM RICE
Music by ANDREW LLOYD WEBBER

Flowing

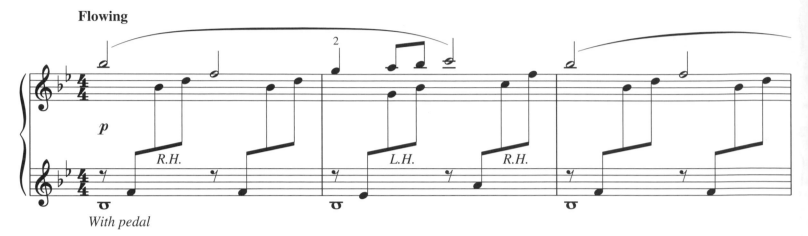

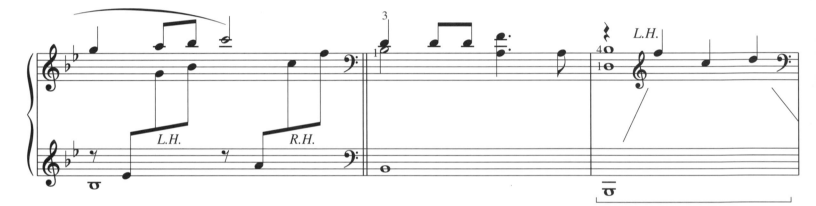

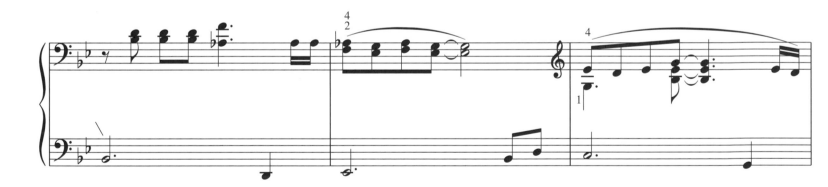

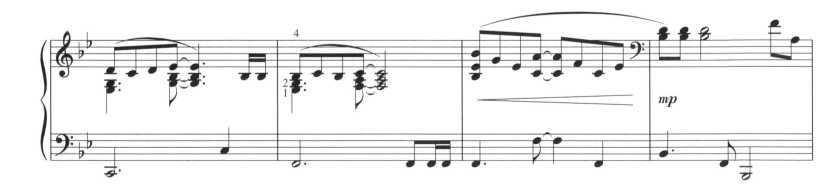

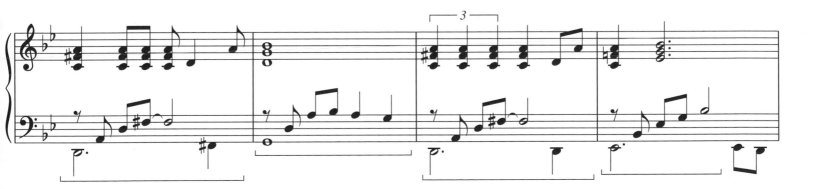

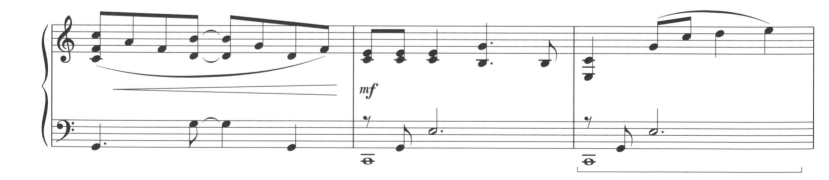

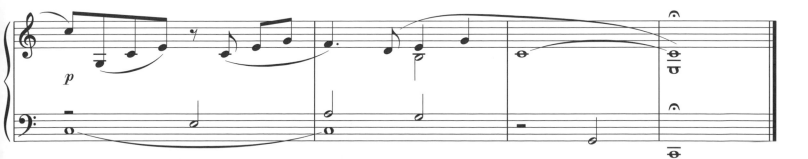